HISTORY AND LORE

There is magic in emeralds, one almost as old as civilization. What a curious human trait to bestow supernatural powers on these tiny jewels born deep within the earth. Perhaps it is the green allure of the earth and of life itself. Or could it be a subliminal response to one of the most restful of colors? Possibly it is the realization that these rare and strangely beautiful crystals were among the first gems people sought and coveted. Before other cultures appreciated diamonds, rubies, or sapphires, early Egyptians mined and fashioned gems at what is generally accepted to be the world's oldest source for emeralds, a site now called Cleopatra's Mines.

NEARLY TWO THOUSAND YEARS BEFORE CLEOPATRA, the mines that bear her name yielded either all or most of the stones used in the earliest emerald jewelry. Literary references are clear, important, and ancient. In the King James version of Exodus, the Breastplate of Judgment is studded with gems, and in "the second row shall be an emerald, a sapphire, and a diamond." And later, in Revelations, gems adorn heaven, "And the foundations of the wall of the city were garnished with all manner of precious stones. The first foundation was jasper; the second sapphire; the third chalcedony; the fourth, an emerald."

Numerous emerald artifacts from cultures as old as 2000 B.C. have been unearthed throughout the Middle East and even Europe (see pages 4, 5, 44). Geologists, anthropologists, and historians wonder whether this one mine was the sole source of emeralds. Since the crystals themselves are as much as a billion years old, the only other cultural curiosity is when people first started using them.

Egyptians mined emeralds in one of the country's least hospitable areas, spread over several miles of desert hills in the Sikait-Zabara region east of Luxor between the Nile and the Red Sea in upper Egypt. No one knows

Colonial Spaniards used many of their Colombian emerald discoveries to adorn religious objects, such as La Lechuga (The Lettuce), an altar piece.

Museum of Gold, Bogotá, Colombia

3

Ancient emerald jewelry appears remarkably contemporary. An unusual Egyptian two-finger ring (above) dates from the first century B.C. Slightly newer, third century A.D. gold dangle Roman earrings feature gem crystals and rabbit cameos.

how actively they worked this area during the empire period, but obviously they found enough material to keep the mines open well over three thousand years. Probably the Romans produced the most during their occupation, when emeralds (such as those in the earrings above) enjoyed great popularity in Italy. Later, Turks and Arabs dug fairly regularly until the thirteenth century and spasmodically into the 1700s, until finally abandoning the depleted mines. A French expedition made an unsuccessful attempt to reopen Cleopatra's Mines in the 1800s. Since then they have remained silent relics in the desert.

These fabled mines raise two intriguing gemological questions. Were these Egyptian stones actually emeralds, and were there other emerald sources? The first century B.C. Egyptian double ring above is itself authentic, but when I was skeptical about its chemistry, the ring's owner had the stone tested. As I suspected, it turned out to be green beryl, which is technically not emerald.

The difference between green beryl and emerald is microscopic trace elements that create distinguishing colors in gems. Emeralds, the brightest and most valuable members of the beryl family, are beryl crystals colored green by chromium, vanadium, or both. Green beryl, usually a duller, less valuable green, is the same chemically, except colored by the presence of iron. Most of the world's aquamarine is actually green beryl heated until it turns blue—the color is caused by a trace of iron. Yellow beryl, called heliodor, and orange or golden beryl also get their tints from iron. Pink beryl, or morganite, and red beryl from Utah, which used to be called bixbite and is now marketed as "red emerald," are most likely colored by manganese.

Obviously not all Egyptian gems have been chemically analyzed, but their general appearance suggests what has historically been called emeralds

The earliest surviving "emerald" jewelry is from the Middle East. Highly prized at the time and referenced in the Bible, most of the above crystals came from deposits in upper Egypt known as Cleopatra's Mines. The unfaceted stones in this Byzantine pendant from the sixth century A.D. would hardly be called gems today. Because of their iron content, most are probably "green beryl," not actually emeralds.

from Cleopatra's Mines may well be green beryl. I have personally never seen any Egyptian stone that has true gem color or quality. Museums typically have on display artifacts like the examples in this chapter—opaque hexagonal crystals drilled and not faceted. Today we call such stones cabochon material, which means gems with enough appeal to be domed but insufficient clarity, transparency, or color to merit faceting.

There is another explanation for the historic references to beautiful, transparent green gems. Before chemists could determine the makeup of crystals, people associated gems by color. Thus, they called all red gems *carbuncles*, whether they were rubies, garnets, or spinels. The word *smaragdus*, which we translate as emerald, was an ancient catchall term for green color. It included a variety of materials—quartz, glass, ceramics, feldspar, and peridot—all later misidentified and mistranslated as emerald. Egypt may well have been the world's original source for beryl crystals (either emerald, green beryl, or both), but the historic and Biblical references to transparent green gems were almost certainly not to emeralds. More likely they referred to peridot, which occurs in large, beautiful crystals that seem to match ancient green gem descriptions. A local peridot source does exist on St. John's island (also called Zabargad) in the Red Sea.

The answer to the second gemological question, were there emerald mines other than Egypt's, is yes. As Roman legions pushed north, they discovered a small deposit in the mountainous Habachtal region of what is now Austria. Unquestionably some Austrian emeralds were worn in Rome, but only a few Roman emerald artifacts look Austrian. Today there are genuine emerald sources in India, Pakistan, and Afghanistan. It is always

6

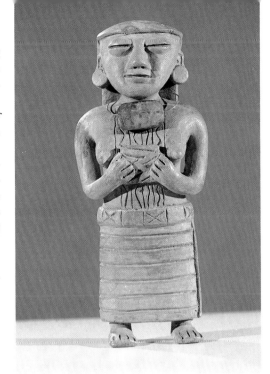

As with gold, silver, jade, and even potatoes, indigenous Indians found and used emeralds before the Spanish arrived in South America. Because everything of value was either melted down or shipped to Spain for sale, few intact artifacts exist as such. The fanciful gold and gem pendant (left), uncovered in Panama, has been described as a bat, jaguar, or crocodile. The drilled emerald crystal and ceramic figure (right), from the Sinú culture in northern Colombia (500-1000 A.D.), were found in a common grave.

Museum of Gold, Bogotá, Colombia

possible that wanderers may have picked up a surface gem or two from these sites over the centuries. But no one has documented any earlier mines in those areas other than the ones opened in the 1940s in India, in the 1960s in Pakistan, or in the 1970s in Afghanistan.

Marco Polo's remarkable journey to China at the end of the thirteenth century added to the saga. He returned with emeralds, as did some of the Crusaders. Were these gems from an unknown mine in one of the three Asian sources, or were they Egyptian emeralds that had been part of the centuries-old trade between Africa and India? I know of no evidence or artifact that suggests another source aside from Egypt and the relatively insignificant find in Austria. I reason that Egypt was both the oldest and the only reliable green beryl or emerald source for the ancient world.

No matter how Egyptian facts emerge, everything else about emeralds dramatically changed in the 1500s. Only then did people outside Central and South America see how large, transparent, and beautiful emeralds could be. What may have been just wishful thinking now became reality. Unknown to the rest of the world, indigenous Indians in what is now Colombia used splendid emerald crystals in jewelry and religious ceremonies for at least 500 years before the Spanish invaded America. As is the case with so much of Spain's conquest of the Americas, the conquistadores came for one thing and left with another.

The avaricious Spanish were obsessed with gold and silver. Spain targeted precious metals in the New World, not jewels, which were commodities the Spanish viewed only as intermediate steps toward acquiring more gold. Jade, which Aztec elite treasured above all other possessions, the

Topkapi Museum, Istanbul

Once the Spanish began trading huge Colombian emeralds, Indian, Turk, and Persian potentates coveted them for their collections. Sometimes they actually instigated wars in order to confiscate gems of rivals.

8

Occasionally rulers offered rare gems as peace gestures. A Turkish sultan ordered the incredible Topkapi Dagger made as a present for the Persian shah. On news of the shah's death, the sultan decided just to keep the gift.

9

No others in history have ever matched Indians' enthusiasm and skill for carving emeralds. India bought Colombia's largest crystals and transformed them into adornments (opposite) for the rich and regal. The great 217 carat **Mogul Emerald** *(left) displays its Shiite prayer with beauty and style. Inscribed and dated in 1695, the tablet has thread openings on all four sides so it could be sewn onto Mogul Emperor Aurangzeb's turban or sleeve for ceremonial occasions.*

The Mogul Emerald, Alan Caplan collection

Spaniards considered worthless green rocks. However, once into Colombia, they realized they had a valuable gem resource to exploit. Although they shared none of India's enthusiasm for green gems, Spanish royalty did engage in a brisk regal traffic, trading their emeralds for gold, diamonds, and pearls.

As Spain sold Colombian emeralds around the globe, kings, queens, and maharajahs assembled huge, lustrous emerald treasures in Europe, India, Turkey, and Persia (Iran). While their collections grew, they attributed to emeralds qualities that became legends, adding to the original Egyptian lore. The amazing Roman chronicler Pliny the Elder described emerald attributes well in his epic work, *Natural History*. "The sight of no other color is more agreeable...because nothing greens greener. Furthermore, they are the only gemstones which fill the eyes without saturating them... eyes will be refreshed and restored by looking at emeralds."

Others ascribed even more astounding properties. Guido Gregorietti wrote, "The emerald...accelerated or retarded the delivery, if attached to the thigh or laid onto the womb of the woman in labor." Various societies claimed other medical successes. Middle Easterners believe that a snake is unlikely to bite anyone wearing an emerald. With a flair for the practical as well as the sublime, Saint Hildegard von Bingen (1098-1179) wrote, "The emerald originates in the early morning at sunrise.... the emerald is a strong remedy against all weakness and disease of man..."

Those born in May are lucky in their birthstone. Emeralds have always been associated with beauty, health, and happiness. Early admirers saw emeralds as the promise of a fresh green spring. Romantics added that emeralds symbolize faith, kindness, and goodness. Dedicating the gems to Venus, they credited emeralds with the power to reveal faithfulness of the beloved. Whatever their other appeals, emeralds' main allure continues to be their look...a unique, pure green to please the eye and soothe the soul.

11

The Hunt for Treasure

Pirates, that's what we are," confided my grizzled friend, whose undetermined heritage matched our seedy surroundings. Sweltering at a filthy table wedged between a row of shantytown brothels and what was overgenerously called an outdoor cafe, we eyed the local gem miners straggling toward a bath and a beer. "Except we don't do pirating on the ocean any more. Instead of burying treasure, we dig for it."

Theirs is not work for the fainthearted, or the lazy, or the security-conscious. I never met a retired gem miner. But this scraggly rabble of adventurers who see pots of gold at the end of every rainbow are responsible for unearthing almost every colored jewel for sale throughout the world. Their lives swing like vast pendulums. Soaring highs and despondent lows sweep them from abject poverty to incredible wealth and back again with dizzying rapidity. Their stories are the stuff of dreams, and nightmares.

NO WHERE IS THE SEARCH FOR GEMS MORE VIOLENT than in Colombia. And no where are the rewards so great, the risks so high, and the treasure itself so magnificent. The quest for Colombian emeralds is everything that gem mining should and should not be.

Details of emerald discovery in the New World have been lost in time, but archaeological dating of various digs reveals Colombian Indians began collecting and fashioning emerald crystals some point after 500 A.D. They mastered drilling early, as witnessed by several large emerald pendant relics, but the indigenous Indians never developed lapidary skills beyond simple shaping. Apparently they never attempted faceting.

Everything related to the history of emeralds and to Indian life changed with the arrival of Christopher Columbus and the Spanish conquistadores who followed in his wake. Finding natives with emeralds, the Spanish sought the mines. It was mid-sixteenth century before they gathered enough information to launch a serious assault on the Indians in the mountains of Colombia north of Bogotá. The Muzos, who controlled the area, fiercely

Part of a day's emerald mining at Muzo fills two hands. The gems are washed and bagged for a helicopter ride to the leaseholder's Bogotá office.

13

protected their heritage. Archaeologists believe the Muzos used emeralds to culminate their annual religious ceremony, when priests immersed their chief, covered with gold and emerald powder, in a nearby lake. The epic struggle between Indians and Spanish soldiers plays on. Descendants of the Muzos and their philosophical brothers, the *guaqueros* who daily dig for emeralds, still have never truly accepted that anyone but them has rights to the gems. As a consequence, the history of Colombian emerald mining has been one of continuous conflict.

MUZO, THE RICHEST AND MOST FAMOUS EMERALD mine in the world, was and is still the main prize. In all my years tramping through gem mines on six continents, I have never seen or heard of any other gem operation like Muzo. It defies logic and reason, and leaves other gem miners gasping in disbelief. And yet, somehow, because of Colombia's history and propensity for fast, atypical solutions, Muzo works sufficiently well to move hundreds of millions of dollars of the world's largest, best, and most beautiful emeralds into the market every year.

Although the national government nominally controls all but one of Colombia's gem mines, Muzo has alternately been privately held, publicly operated, and even once owned by a British firm. Currently the government issues a ten year lease to work the 200 hectares (500 acres) that comprise the main Muzo deposit, for which it charges only a million-dollar-a-year royalty. Bogotá-based Tecminas holds that lease until 1994. The down side—to operate Muzo, Tecminas employees live and work in an armed camp.

I travelled to Muzo by Tecminas helicopter, not for luxury or scenery, but because I wanted to get there alive. Bandits make two assumptions about motor traffic to and from Muzo. If you are heading in, you must

Muzo, the world's most famous and valuable emerald mine, looks like a coal deposit. Setting the standard for size, color, quality, and price, Muzo's emeralds form in calcite veins running vertically through black shale. The Colombian government sells a ten year lease to the main site, but anyone with enough nerve can mine the inky streams that flow below the company's guarded compound.

15

be carrying money to buy emeralds. If you are heading out, you must be carrying emeralds. Either way, you are fair game. When I asked about this danger, a government official told me that *bandidos* had even ambushed an armed fifty jeep supply convoy, killing eight Tecminas workers.

At first look Muzo appears to be a giant coal mine. The raw exposed point at the confluence of Animas Stream, Itoco River, and Minero River used to define a steep valley. Miners over the centuries have discarded millions of tons of black shale tailings into the streams, actually raising the level of the valley floor over 70 meters. The black shale mountain holds hydrothermally formed emeralds secreted in calcite cavities. Uncover crystallized white calcite veins, which usually run vertically, and you expose emeralds. It is deceptively simple, inexpensive surface or strip mining. But the Colombian solution for Muzo is uniquely convoluted.

Since the shale is soft and the emeralds near the surface, bulldozers make repetitive swipes at the face. Each of the mine's 200 employees receives an average of only $160 a month in wages, but they fight for jobs to get the revolving fringe benefit—*picando*, one day a month of free pickups. Every day's work crew surrounds the bulldozer, on the lookout for calcite. At the first flash of white, the workers dash to the wall and begin digging out emeralds with their hands and small picks. A representative of the families that control Tecminas inspects their finds, holding out the ones he wants for the mine. The individuals are then allowed to pocket the remainder as a bonus for working at Muzo!

After that Tecminas makes no further attempt to search the tons of shale scraped aside. Instead, workers bulldoze all that emerald-bearing dirt

Occasionally Colombian miners find an emerald crystal still attached to the calcite matrix where it formed (left). Collectors and museums avidly seek gem quality specimen.

One of the finest crystals ever unearthed came from Colombia's Coscuez mine. The government considers this 1,759 carat beauty (right) too nearly perfect to cut. With a naturally flat terminated top and hexagonal sides, the gem is one of five emerald giants held in the national bank in Bogotá.

Bank of the Republic, Bogotá, Colombia

over the side of the hill toward 5,000 to 30,000 expectant *guaqueros* who jam the stream beds below, picking through the black shale that falls their way.

A dark crucible of human frailties, the tiny area is a dangerous mix of gems, alcohol, desperation, and jealousies over women and territory. Colombians may freely work the tailings, but, as a testimony to the risks, on average one to five *guaqueros* a week die in the streams and surrounding shanties. In contrast to this frequent fratricide, an uneasy truce exists between the *guaqueros* and Tecminas, looming above. A fenced and surrounded outpost, Muzo reminds me of Vietnam. Vigilant against intruders, workers with rifles and pistols patrol the perimeter.

Muzo and two other mines, Chivor and Coscuez, supply the vast majority of Colombian emeralds, but there are many other smaller operations. Although not the largest volume producer, Colombia accounts for over half the world's annual billion dollar wholesale emerald market because of the crystal size and quality of its unprecedented emerald riches.

B razil, best known for the diversity of its gorgeous colored gems, is the world's largest volume emerald producer. Obviously overshadowed by Colombia and Zambia as high-end sources, Brazil nevertheless often surprises buyers with emeralds larger than 200 carats (page 20). Jewelry manufacturers in Rio use many of the better stones for their highly competitive local tourist trade. However, most of Brazil's commercial gems go to India for cutting, then to Hong Kong and Thailand for setting into relatively inexpensive jewelry. Unlike name recognition for Burma rubies and Colombian emeralds, Brazil's gems sell anonymously in the marketplace.

Gem mining is typically labor intensive. Most mines are in remote areas of Third World countries where it is cheaper to dig and separate by hand rather than buy and maintain machines. At Brazil's Nova Era mine, prospectors wash away unwanted gravel to pick out gems.

Brazilian prospector-miners, *garimpeiros*, first discovered green crystals in the 1960s, but geologists quarreled over what to call the stones. They were beryl all right, but colored by a trace of the element vanadium. Many in the gem trade refused to recognize as emerald any beryl not colored green by chromium. Brazilian miners and dealers fought for acceptance until the Gemological Institute of America, the world's best known and most respected gemological organization, issued a lab report in 1963 identifying vanadium-colored stones from Salininha, Brazil, as "natural emerald."

Now most experts agree that emeralds may be colored by either chromium or vanadium, or both. Tests show that many emeralds also have trace amounts of iron. For me the distinguishing factor is appearance. If a beryl crystal is emerald green, no matter what trace element produces the green, then I think it should be labeled emerald.

Brazilians have crowded a great deal of controversy into their short emerald mining history. The government flooded the Salininha mine for a hydroelectric project. Depending on local disputes, the country's newest mine, Nova Era, oscillates between open and closed. But two areas yield the huge amounts needed to maintain Brazil's position as volume leader. To the northeast, Carnaiba appears to have one of the world's largest emerald deposits in the world. And north of Brasilia, miners riddle the red rolling hills around Santa Teresinha with hundreds of unsupported tunnels, often exceeding 100 meters deep. Here more than 20,000 people earn their living daily digging for emeralds.

Africa is increasingly important as an emerald producer. Like Brazil, several East African countries supply emeralds colored by vanadium. Zambia

Rough emeralds come in many shapes and sizes. The huge 380 carat crystal (left) was an early find at Brazil's newest mine near Nova Era. Usually, such mines produce both large and small stones in every conceivable shape. An exception was Brazil's Salininha mine, which produced almost uniform small sized hexagonal emerald rods (right).

has an enviable reputation for mining large, relatively clean gems that command very high market prices. But like so many other newly independent African countries, Zambia has trouble maintaining a consistent government policy toward gem mining or even holding onto the emeralds it finds.

IN AN ATTEMPT TO MINIMIZE THEFT and increase profits, Zambia recently had a unique five-year joint venture with Maurice Roditi, Brazil's third largest gem dealer. The government wanted control of Zambia's emerald mining by prohibiting rough and polished exports. It imported fifty Brazilians to cut all emeralds in a new factory and train a corps of African cutters. Roditi had worldwide marketing rights, but once the Brazilians succeeded at faceting and selling, Zambia nationalized the operation.

Depending on whose figures you believe, about half the emeralds mined still leave Zambia without benefit of papers or taxes, assisted by the most unlikely band of smugglers ever assembled to facilitate what many in the trade call the world's oldest profession. From their ancestral home on the other side of the continent, Senegalese tribesmen roam East Africa paying hard currency cash for stolen emeralds. Starting near the government's Kagem mine in northern Zambia, the Senegalese carry their loot by foot to Zaire, then fly to Geneva to bargain with the world's emerald buyers. Whether they sell directly to Israeli factories and dealers or European middlemen, the result is the same—Israelis in Tel-Aviv end up faceting a large percentage of uncut Zambian rough.

Further south in Zimbabwe, in perhaps the most efficient of all emerald mines, England's Rio Tinto successfully employs First World mining technology and security in a Third World environment. Sandawana is both underground and profitable, an unusual combination for colored gem mines. It produces bright, clean, highly desirable small emeralds that hold their color in the tiny sizes needed to *pavé* jeweled watch faces and cluster

Almost as many guards watch as workers clean and sort emeralds. Even though the Zambian government maintains a considerable security presence at its Kagem mine, the better emeralds still seem to find their way to the black market.

Zambia, one of the world's three most important emerald suppliers, mines many large gems with relatively few inclusions. But a gray tint in Zambian emeralds (apparently caused by vanadium) makes them less valuable than Colombia's best.

Zambia produces emeralds from both government (above) and private mines (left). However, the results are similar. The government has difficulty controlling its finds. Few of the gems unearthed at private mines are reported or taxed. Legal exports usually sell directly to Israel. Smuggled goods go first to Switzerland before moving to Israeli cutters.

jewelry. As with all other colored gems, color deepens as the stone size increases. In sizes smaller than 2mm, emeralds from most countries, including Colombia, usually look very pale. Sandawana is most popular as a supplier of emeralds that remain dark green even in small accent stone sizes.

Other African countries, such as Mozambique, Madagascar, and Tanzania, also mine, but Zambia and Zimbabwe produce the majority of African emeralds. To the east another pair of countries are having difficulties finding their places in the emerald market.

In Pakistan's rugged Himalayan foothills, workers battle difficult terrain and weather to operate two mines, Mingora and Gujar Kili. The mine in Mingora is the exception for Pakistan and for gem mines generally. Located in town, it would be overrun by prospectors and claim jumpers almost anywhere else. But the deposit was discovered in the 1960s while the Wadi of Swat ruled the area. He dealt with gem theft harshly. When Pakistan took control, there was never a question about public access.

Gujar Kili may be the most beautifully situated gem mine anywhere. Isolated on a ledge above a steep roadless valley, it is reachable only by a footpath that meanders beside and across the lovely Kotkai River. Although breathtakingly scenic, the unmechanized mine produces almost nothing—

Whatever the source, the goal is the same, to find marketable gems. One of the best crystals ever recovered at the small, noncommercial U.S. deposit near Hiddenite, North Carolina, (left) weighs 111 carats. Pakistanis dig most emeralds by hand (above). Their government operates two mines in the Valley of Swat. Others, located at higher, usually frozen elevations, are unprofitable even to open.

The British Museum (Natural History)

only 30,000 to 40,000 carats annually, an amount Muzo probably tops every week. At 6200 feet, Gujar Kili has to close part of every winter. The Pakistanis have prospected several other emerald deposits too high in the frozen Himalayas to mine.

Across the Khyber Pass in the Panjsher Valley, Afghans work under some of the worst conditions anywhere. In addition to enduring punishing altitudes and climate, miners suffer from the continuing civil war that has plagued Afghanistan for years. They transport their limited emerald supplies on foot to market in Peshawar, Pakistan.

To the north, in the Ural Mountains, Russians let lie an emerald deposit of unknown dimensions. After the 1830s discovery, czars ordered emerald mines worked only spasmodically. For the last half century the communist government mined the area, not for gems but beryllium, needed to process nuclear material. Whether the new Russian state will develop the resource as it has done with Siberian diamonds remains an open question.

Gem mining may seem an anachronism in modern society. Hordes of men in dozens of countries drive huge machines and endure some of the riskiest, most miserable working conditions imaginable in their endless quest for tiny, elusive, colorful crystals. Few question this wisdom. The reward is so great—to uncover a priceless piece of time, a natural rarity, a gem.

ROMANCING
THE STONE

Balancing on the edge of a small ledge, I watched the groaning bulldozer below. Its glistening steel blade scraped away a few inches of pure black shale beneath my feet. When black turned white, the dozen or so men who surrounded the 'dozer dashed toward the exposed calcite veins, grasping for emeralds. I saw the glint of green and sensed the thrill of discovery. Emeralds buried under Muzo's hills for millions of years since their birth reflected the sun for the first time.

Though fascinating to gemologists and collectors, such stones are not marketable to the public in uncut form. An amazing array of skills, a great deal of money, and a surprising number of people work their magic to enhance the ultimate moment when the customer slips this perfect creation of nature onto a ring finger.

Whether we discover small broken fragments, cloudy lumps that can only be cabochons, or great transparent crystals fabulous for centerstones, we possess an innate human need to alter nature's masterpieces to match our dreams. We apply the accumulated knowledge of 7,000 years to shape them into precious treasures, a process I call *Romancing the Stone*.

Consider what was available to the first gem collectors and what they did with their finds. Early humans who overturned pretty, bright crystals unquestionably liked them just as they came from the ground. More attractive and harder than rocks being used as tools, crystals were durable, beautiful, and almost always rare—and thus valuable. Those traits remain today as the three most important factors to define gems.

GEMS HAVE TO BE SEEN TO BE APPRECIATED. Our ancestors surely found that walking around carrying crystals in their pouches or bags defeated much of the reason for owning them. Amazingly, after nearly 100,000 years, almost every group had solved their common desire to wear

For movie queens like Elizabeth Taylor, whose exquisite taste in personal jewelry is reflected in this suite of Colombian emeralds, owning gems is both a pleasure and a great investment. Famous owners enjoy a lifetime of use while their fame contributes to increased gem values.

their finds in basically the same way. Whether with natural pearls near Bahrain, rubies in India, or emeralds in Colombia, early people learned that by simply drilling holes they created necklace and pendant beads. Hole drilling was the initial move toward jewelry making.

Of all the things people now do to render gems wearable and attractive, most alterations fall into two categories: reshaping (which includes fashioning and faceting) and enhancing. Since crystal collectors, geologists, mineralogists, and gemologists are among the few who enjoy crystals in their natural form, dealers have most gems cut to make them more appealing to a wider public. The practice of cutting is old, but mastery of the techniques came late in human development.

Gems and jewelry unearthed throughout north Africa and the Middle East prove people shaped and drilled crystals before 3,000 B.C. From relics found intact, it seems early emeralds were usually just drilled (see pages 4, 5, 39, 44) while many other gems were roughly shaped or domed into cabochons. Old cutters did little more than control overall gem contours.

Diamond discoveries in India about 500 B.C. inspired people to cut gemstones. It was easy for potentates to love the unmatched hardness of the new gems, but the colorless crystals must have looked bland and a bit glassy as they came from the alluvial flats near Golconda. Early Indian cutters

28

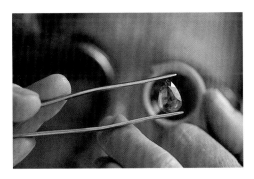

Once mined, gemstones usually change hands several times. In Santa Teresinha, Brazil, as elsewhere, the first sale often begins in an open air street market (left). Miners or their agents offer washed crystals to seated buyers. A few dealers, such as those from H. Stern, Roditi Jewelers, and Amsterdam Sauer (below right), are important enough in the market to have their own buying offices. Back in Rio, new Brazilian emeralds are faceted, graded, and priced (above right). Most Rio firms sell both loose stones as well as finished jewelry.

started a process we now recognize as the first steps to faceting. They shaped diamonds, putting a few flat surfaces on the larger crystals to reflect light to the viewer. But even the great Indian diamonds looked lifeless until European cutters refaceted them during the last few hundred years. Unfortunately, many precious gems had already been ruined by inept handling.

Renaissance Europeans contributed their scientific advances and mechanical abilities to centuries of lapidary skills. In their hands what was rough craft became humanistic art. Cutting and polishing with imported diamond grit and emery, they applied new light gathering and reflection concepts to old grinding techniques. The Europe of their day burgeoned with world trade, art, and science. Colonial conquests produced gems, and out of their vast treasuries, wealthy rulers commissioned great personal adornments. During the next 500 years, jewelers mastered faceting—the angles, numbers, and placement of tiny flat polished reflective surfaces that make gems sparkle.

Paralleling these fashioning and faceting advances was a far less obvious and less understood aspect of stone romancing. Treating gems to make them more attractive may not be as old as human history, but it is close. While researching my *Rubies & Sapphires* book, I found gems treated by the

most ancient of all enhancements, heating, as early as 2000 B.C. Our friend Pliny the Elder wrote that his contemporaries in ancient Rome practiced the chicanery of sorcerers with a rich brew of gem tricks and enhancements, including heating, reflective foil backs, dyeing, and glass substitution.

Most of today's emerald buyers make shape their first decision. Of all the possible geometries—oval, round, heart, pear, marquise—the traditional emerald cut (or octagon) is the most popular, particularly with conservative and first time buyers. The emerald cut suits the hexagonal crystal and its refractive index, delivering a good yield as well as a beautiful look. Unlike round brilliant cuts for diamonds, which are calculated for maximum reflection, emerald cuts emphasize a gem's color depth. Rather than seeing reflections from the stone, emerald cuts encourage you to experience the gem's richness by actually looking into the crystal. After exploring the subtle depths of greens, you can then study the unique inclusions that give emeralds character.

"INCLUSIONS," OR INTERNAL CHARACTERISTICS, are all the extras that appear in gem crystals. They may be fractures, trapped liquids, growth lines, embedded crystals of other materials, gas, cavities, spots, specks, or a host of other microscopic occurrences that some consider flaws and others call beauty marks. Whatever your disposition, inclusions are a fact of life with emeralds. Separate from diamond clarity grades, the GIA

Hundreds of thousands of Indian cutters facet most of the world's smaller, less expensive emeralds, mainly Brazilian stones. To assure a constant trained labor supply, Jaipur factories operate a gem school (right) in what was the maharani's palace. Hand-powered bow strings turn cutting and polishing wheels (left) throughout the central Indian gem center. One type emerald is cut no where else—tiny, 142-per-carat faceted jewels (above) that are used to decorate expensive Swiss watch faces.

Inclusions, which are considered flaws by some observers and unique, identifying and even attractive characteristics by others, are expected features in emeralds. They are visible reminders of each gem's birth experience. Trace elements, trapped debris, and stress-induced fissures are all frozen records of crystal creation hundreds of millions of years ago. The sugar-loaf cab from Colombia's Muzo mine (below, left and page 62) shows many particles, while the Madagascar pear-shape (below, right) has both a microscopic precipitate as well as numerous fractures.

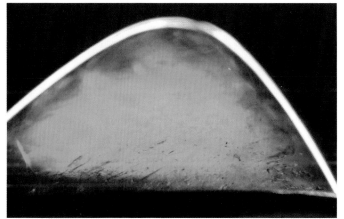

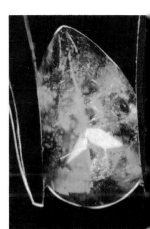

Equatorian Imports, Dallas

Braving what is increasingly hazardous duty, American dealers Ray and Sheila Falvo Zajicek make several buying trips to Colombia each year. Ray says he takes the risk because "the selection is better and I like the action." Most U.S. dealers prefer waiting at home until Colombian sellers arrive with emeralds. In contrast, several hundred Japanese emerald buyers operate full time in Colombia.

categorizes three clarity types for colored gems:

Type I gemstones, "often virtually inclusion-free," such as aquamarine, citrine, topaz, green tourmaline, and tanzanite.

Type II gems, "usually included," the majority of crystals, such as rubies, sapphires, garnets, peridot, amethyst, spinel, most tourmalines, and zircons.

Type III gemstones, "almost always included," principally red tourmalines and emeralds .

There is considerable speculation about the cause of the most obvious emerald inclusions, though not much scientific evidence. I will therefore venture an opinion based on years of observations. Two major gems, emeralds and rubies, get their color from the presence of chromium. Other varieties of the same gems (white sapphires, which are sisters to rubies; and aquamarine, morganite, green and yellow beryl, emeralds' siblings) often are mined without inclusions. Vanadium-colored emeralds do not have as many inclusions as chromium-colored samples. Therefore, I think that oversized chromium atoms stress gem crystals to produce what the French call *jardin*, a garden of inclusions that gives emeralds their visual character.

Oiling emeralds to mask natural inclusions is often very effective and certainly routine. As a rule, the buying public does not realize their emeralds are oiled because the trade does not disclose the practice or outright denies that oiling is common. Now that you know most emeralds are oiled several times between mine and market, you can buy with greater understanding of the process and later know how to care for your emeralds.

Oiling is an almost universal emerald enhancement, but virtually unknown to the public. Of all the major gems, emeralds are most likely to have inclusions, distinctive relics of the crystals' birth process. Some serve as fingerprints, by which gemologists identify naturals. Too many inclusions diminish a stone's beauty and value. Oiling is not permanent and should be repeated every few years. Only if cracks reach the surface can an emerald benefit from oiling.

A Bogotá laboratory technician washes and dries emeralds (top). Then he soaks them overnight in heated oil, sometimes under pressure, to force oil into inclusions (left). After draining and another cleaning, some emeralds display substantial improvement. Shown above is a 28 ct. gem before and after oiling. Usually, whoever owns a gem at the time it is faceted decides whether to oil.

Early oiling has two purposes: to make emeralds more salable to the wholesale market, and to help cutters plan their work. Some factories store rough emeralds in buckets of oil prior to cutting. At this point there is no intent to fool buyers or beautify the material. Cutters simply need to assess what inclusions have to be dealt with before faceting. A handful of unoiled rough looks dull and opaque. Not very revealing. But, soaked in mineral oil, the stones turn darker, more colorful, and transparent enough to see inside.

Since oiling is easy, inexpensive, and almost universal, I am continually intrigued when clients declare, "I don't want to buy an oiled emerald," or "I know my emerald isn't oiled." No dealer has any control over whether emeralds are oiled. Within an hour of cutting in Colombia or Brazil, the gem's owner has it in an oiling lab. The stone has to attract a buyer to get the gem into the world market. Fewer visible inclusions mean quicker sales at better prices. This overnight oiling process is omitted only if no inclusions reach the surface. Inclusions that reach the surface serve as a conduit so oil can fill internal inclusions.

There are almost as many oils as there are Chinese herbal medicines. For rough emeralds the most widely used are baby or mineral oil, linseed oil, and the ever popular household "3 in 1" machine oil. For faceted gems the witch's brew may also consist of personal favorites and "family secrets." The trade considers only green oils unethical. Large labs offer clients a choice, including cedarwood, balsam, and palm. Brazilian oilers favor a heavier household plastic sealer, Opticon, because it lasts longer than oil, but some dealers feel it is cloudier and more visible. Israeli treaters use a heavier material like Opticon, but keep its chemistry secret.

Most great emeralds are oiled. Only a gemologist or a gem lab can tell for sure. Oil usually evaporates within two to five years. Since heat speeds the process, a sunny desert climate is the most drying. If your emerald looks more included than when you bought it, have it reoiled. Treat reoiling as routinely as you do restringing pearls.

Although emeralds are hard, in fact, harder than some steel, they are almost always included. Therefore, they can be vulnerable to chipping, particularly where inclusions intersect the surface.

Another concern is toughness, which means resistance to breakage. In addition to possible chipping, emeralds are not as tough as jade and some other gems. To protect your investment, when making or repairing jewelry, choose an emerald specialist to design your setting and mount your stones. Jewelers who may be extremely competent with diamonds must take extra precautions with emeralds. Ask to make sure your setter has emerald experience. If you buy good stones, set them well, and wear them carefully, you can expect a lifetime of beauty.

Dealers Ed Swoboda and Osorio Neto successfully bid $350,000 for the first major lot from Nova Era, a new Brazilian emerald mine. Included in their 6500 carats was a single 380 carat crystal. Every choice they made on cut, size, and shape affected profits.

JEWELS AND ARTIFACTS

W hy do you suppose today's women love to buy and wear gems while today's men seem only to tolerate the purchases?" I often direct this question to my gem talk audiences. Not an idle query for those of us who both appreciate gems and sell them. "And who has owned and worn the most impressive jewels throughout history?" The typical answer from the crowd, "Queens and movie stars."

That has not always been the case. For as long as anyone knows, jewels have been beautiful symbols of wealth and power. Royalty controlled them all. Except for a few historical anomalies, such as Cleopatra, Queen Victoria and the Elizabeths, royalty meant kings. For thousands of years of human history, male rulers lusted after gemstones, started wars to loot treasures others had mined, and proudly flaunted their conquests by adorning themselves with their bounty. Kings and people favored by kings owned gems and transformed them into the visual status symbols of their power—crowns, scepters, and other regal paraphernalia. Before paper money and stock certificates, people measured wealth by their land, their jewels, and their gold. It used to be unthinkable that common people and especially common women would ever own and wear such treasures.

Today we have a topsy-turvy gem market. Ownership has obviously changed over the last 150 years. The Industrial Revolution, a vast social upheaval that moved people from farms to factories, coincided with the exploration of the world's far corners, which brought more gem discoveries. Simultaneously, a global wave of independence and two World Wars swept away kingdoms and colonies. People earned salaries instead of shares in crops. The new buying power of this burgeoning middle class and the increased supplies gave rise to what I call the *Democratization of Gems.*

Working people wanted and could now afford what had been the perquisites of royalty. Simultaneously, huge new diamond discoveries, first in

Mel Fisher found the Atocha, part of Spain's hapless treasure fleet sunk by a hurricane off Florida in 1622. Among the recovered booty was this exquisite emerald cross (left), which fetched $1.3 million. Most gemstones then were merely rounded into cabochons.

Bank Melli, Tehran

Topkapi Palace Museum

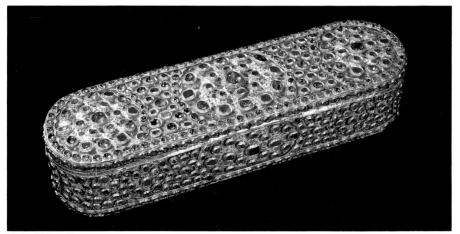

Topkapi Palace Museum

38

Regal trinkets....

Emerald use and marketing changed totally after Spain's conquest of Colombia in the 1500s. Suddenly spectacular gems were available in Europe, which had no history of appreciating them. But the rulers of India, Persia, and Turkey certainly knew how to showcase the new finds. India, as the conduit, fought wars for control of the fabulous jewels. Great crystals were drilled for beads (above), placed in necklaces, and set in elaborate pieces to decorate thrones (below, center).

Royalty garnered jewels, often lost, then regained them. Huge collections in Turkey and Iran remain substantially intact in museums, but the Indian government forced maharajahs to sell their treasures after independence in 1948. The last Shah of Iran reused "antique" emeralds in new crowns (opposite, top left). The Iranian Crown Jewels also feature what has sometimes been described as the world's most beautiful gem creation, an all emerald and diamond box (opposite, center). Turkish sultans held audiences beneath gigantic emerald crystals suspended over their thrones (opposite, top right) and kept their writing materials in an emerald and ruby encrusted gold container (opposite, bottom).

R. Esmerian

Topkapi Palace Museum

R. Esmerian

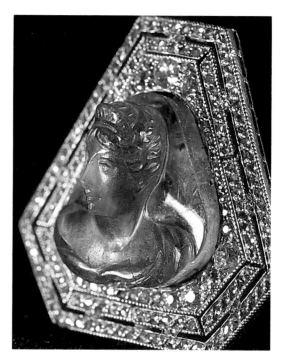

Ted Hotovitz collection

Egyptians, Greeks, and Romans carved and engraved emeralds, but the then available Egyptian material was poorly suited for carving. Few examples remain. After the 16th century Colombian emerald discoveries, artists in India mastered gem carving (see page 10).

South Africa, later in Russia and Australia, supplied far more gems than royalty or the privileged could absorb. De Beers, the diamond mining and marketing syndicate, created a massive, worldwide jewel promotion directed at this new buying group. As anyone who has seen the advertisements knows, the De Beers' campaign convinced men to buy gems for women.

Ironically, now that gems are universally available, many American men shy away from wearing them and mainly buy for women. Almost no engagement would be complete today without a diamond. By the same token, the bride usually reciprocates with a gold band instead of a gemstone ring. The dichotomy between what women and men consider appropriate to wear is, I believe, cultural, not genetic. The depth of people's love for gems attests to their primal appeal. But many of today's Western men apparently suppress their innate appreciation. This historical shift from men being the principal owners and wearers of gems to today's apprehension may be an area ripe for anthropologists instead of gem writers.

I tell clients there are many tasteful, manly designs. Some make powerful statements. If a man worries that a gemstone ring may not be right for him, I suggest we incorporate a strong, simple shape to give him a look of authority. Cabochons and sugar-loaf cuts effectively avoid faceting, which we usually couple with women's jewelry. Men in other countries continue to buy

Carving skills next developed in 18th and 19th century Europe, resulting in a wide variety of jewelry. The man's portrait, far left, was used as a tie tack while the later empress' bust was made into a pin. An Art Deco ring (above, left) contains an image of Satyr while Homer graces another tie tack (above, right).

gems for themselves. Some men associate jewelry wearing with negative stereotypes in our society (such as drug dealers), who are often portrayed on television draped in gold. To heighten their appeal, I point out that fine gems do not fluctuate in value with the wild swings we see in the stock market.

Investing in gems is a topic that surfaces almost every time I talk. The buyer is generally interested in money, the wearer in beauty. Women in the audience often want to know where to shop, how to buy wisely, and how to care for their gems. Now that men are not the principal gem wearers, they concentrate on the investment value of their purchases. Even though gems do appreciate, I rarely suggest buying them solely as an investment. Better to buy them as a token of love or as a marker for life's peak experiences. Ponder alternative tangible gifts, such as furs, flowers, or automobiles, which rapidly age and depreciate. In contrast, gems are perfect pieces of nature, crystalline wonders already hundreds of millions of years old and likely to be even more valuable after decades of enjoyment. They are perennial—ancient and timeless.

Lower quality gems, semiprecious stones, and costume jewelry may just keep up with inflation; but fine quality colored gems, such as emeralds, rubies, and sapphires, usually rise in value. (Diamonds are in a different category because De Beers controls their market.) The reasons for gem

Roditi Jewelers

Five emerald rings ranging in size from two to sixteen carats and in price from $14,000 to $75,000 were all designed and made in Brazil. High quality emeralds often wholesale for more then $25,000 a carat.

appreciation are logical and stable, even in our fast changing world. There is a finite supply of all gems and an ever diminishing number of new fine stones. It is one of the exasperating aspects of mining that the very best material always seems to be extracted early in a mine's life. No one knows why there have been no recent Muzo emeralds as fabulous as the ones in the Crown Jewels of Iran, at the Topkapi in Istanbul, or in the Smithsonian. It is unlikely that another find will soon flood the world with gems. Such a bonanza has happened only a few times throughout history.

Are gems a good investment? It depends on your circumstances. For some people, gems are the only reasonable investment. As the U.S.S.R., China, and Eastern Europe all open to the West and capitalism, one of the first things their workers will buy is gems. Vanity does not lead stressed societies to jewels. People who fear their paper money may become worthless turn to the traditional form of transportable wealth that worked for their ancestors. In the U.S. we seldom think of portability as a reason for buying gems. But for much of the world, the prospect of their investments (money, stocks, homes, property) suddenly becoming worthless is a very real threat. People running for their lives do not run with gold or

42

Even though Brazil is a large producer of emeralds, its fine jewelers also use foreign gems for the country's tourist and domestic markets. The center emerald is Zambian and the other four are all Colombian.

paper money. When possible they flee today as they have for millennia, with the most compact of all the world's currencies, gems.

In the less threatened West, gems can be solid investments if you buy well. Recent comparisons of wholesale price rises for a variety of stones over the past twenty years show emeralds up 1500%, diamonds up 1456%, and sapphires up 1186%. The greater premium you pay, the longer it will take to recover your investment. I advise you to comparison shop. Large and fine quality investment grade gems require the same buying care and expertise as other major purchases. However, gems, like real estate, are not necessarily liquid. If you aim to increase value, set a goal, buy quality, and be able to wait.

A friend of mine bought a very good colored gem in the 1960s for well under $100,000, still a fancy price in those days; then he waited. Less than thirty years later he sold it for over $3 million, an incredible profit. Can his success be repeated? Of course. At the same time that the number of fine new colored gems either remains the same or diminishes, the number of available gem buyers in the world grows exponentially. Demand for quality stones has seldom been higher. Will it be common? No. But if you buy at a good, honest price and take care of your gem, it will certainly be worth a great deal more

A thousand years of emerald jewelry are represented in two necklaces. Separated by half a world, two cultures found and treasured emerald crystals, but neither had the tools or skills to facet gems. Above, emeralds (or green beryl) from upper Egypt's mines accent a beautifully preserved necklace from third century B.C. Carthage. Early Middle Eastern craftsmen used hexagonal emeralds as they came from the ground, simply drilling a single hole for stringing.

In the New World (right), pre-Colombian Indians also drilled single holes, but their purpose was to make pendants.

44

in thirty years than it is today. And you won't have to feed it, paint it, or manage it. You can sleep nights without wondering if its value is going up or down with the Dow. Most importantly, you or someone you love will have enjoyed wearing it for those thirty years. Investments never get much better than this. Ever gaze in admiration at a stock certificate?

Many people ask me if the color of their emeralds will last. Although morganite, kunzite, and some amethyst do fade after prolonged exposure to bright light, the vast majority of gem colors are permanent. The reason most objects we own fade is that they are colored by dyes that react mainly to the ultraviolet energy in sunlight. By contrast, the colors we see in gemstones are not the result of dyes but the molecular structure of the crystal acting like a light filter. The emerald you own, like all the members of the beryl gem family, is beryllium aluminum silicate. Without chromium, a beryl crystal is colorless. But with less than one percent chromium (or vanadium), the crystal lattice passes the green portion of white light while absorbing red and blue. Whenever you see an emerald, you see green. And the green you love today will still be there when the sun dies.

L ooking at the numerous emerald artifacts of various cultures throughout history leaves us many unanswered questions. It seems clear that Egypt was the oldest emerald source (assuming that some of the material was emerald and not green beryl). Certainly, over several thousand years, traders would have dispersed those crystals throughout the Middle East and into India. And a great number of written accounts (Biblical, Roman, and others) describe incredible specimen, objects, individual gems, and even building columns as emeralds. Emerald crystals do not age, are not affected by time, desert heat, cold, or dry conditions. If they ever existed, where are the artifacts? And why have we found no great emeralds from the Egyptian tombs that produced many other of the finest preserved treasures in history?

I have pieced together a logical answer. People used to categorize gems by color, not chemistry. Before analytic techniques, if an object were green, cut nicely, set in gold, and owned by someone important, it was fairly easy to call it emerald. In addition to finding several errors in Pliny's emerald accounts, beryl expert John Sinkankas identifies the famous emerald "Holy Grail" in Genoa as merely glass. Other relics have turned out to be chrysoprase, jasper, enamel, peridot, and more recently plastic and ceramic.

People may lose or discard medium quality possessions over time. Seldom do they misplace great gems. Egypt probably produced few, if any, good emeralds, which would explain a lack of fine emerald artifacts. Archaeologists and grave diggers have found only small opaque crystals. Notice the dramatic differences between the Egyptian crystals on pages 4, 5, and 44 and the newer, larger, transparent Colombian emeralds throughout this chapter. Although they have historic value, the Egyptian material seen in these pages could not be sold today as gems. It is remotely possible that if a specimen survived in its original form until the Renaissance, it might have been faceted, and thus would be unrecognizable as Egyptian. However, modern testing techniques can reveal true sources, and no one to my knowledge has ever identified an Egyptian stone comparable to modern gems.

With emeralds, the unusual is commonplace. When England ruled India, British officials and wealthy merchants often adopted some of the maharajahs' princely habits, including sporting fancy gems. The head of the East India Company had this personal seal ring carved with his name and the date 1797 in reverse type. Today it would be almost unthinkable to carve emeralds such as this. In some ways it is an aesthetic loss to the world that dealers facet almost all fine gemstones because faceting assures higher profits.

Occasionally emeralds from only a few mines in Colombia grow in a unique shape, six separate crystals joined to a central core. Called trapiches, the Spanish word for cogwheels in sugar mills, these rare configurations are prized by a devoted group of collectors. Cutters almost never facet trapiches. Instead, they smooth them into cabochons for pendants, earrings, rings, and pins. Several gems have spawned similar relatively unknown collection specialties. A few select buyers seek naturally colored diamonds and larger, flawless specimen. Sapphire collectors want the unusual colors, color-change jewels, and fine large blue stones from Kashmir and Burma. Besides trapiches, emerald collectors covet well shaped crystals in matrix, the native rock where they formed.

Victoria and Albert Museum, London

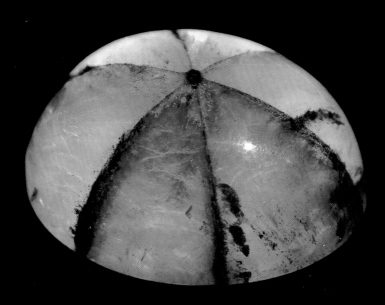

The Star of the Andes trapiche emerald, 80.61 carats; Powerstones, Austin

Is it possible that some of the ancient gem writers might have described emeralds from India, Russia, Afghanistan, or Pakistan? We know from discoveries in the 1800s and 1900s that all four countries have emerald deposits and that early people lived or traveled around the deposit sites. The occasional gem pickup was always possible. However, I found no relics or analyses suggesting that any emeralds prior to Spain's opening of Colombia in the mid-1500s came from any source other than Egypt or Austria.

Yet, if relics in museums and private collections that have been analyzed are representative, then we have to conclude that historic emeralds were typically small and less than gem quality. In fact, it is not farfetched to say that people probably never saw high quality emeralds until the discoveries in Colombia. What makes these relatively late finds even more amazing is that the Spanish adventurers targeted the Colombian mines because they felt emeralds might be valuable. They had no way of knowing that what they were about to seize was the world's first true gem emerald mine, with jewels far more valuable than their beloved gold.

India has the grandest of all histories with both diamonds and colored gems. With a large population in place and a collection of maharajahs ruling individual states, Indians were the world's leading gem market for thousands of years. They were also fortunate to have a great variety, including diamonds, rubies, garnets, natural pearls, and sapphires from what used to be Ceylon and is now Sri Lanka. When jewels were found elsewhere, such as rubies and sapphires in Burma, India bought them too. With an intensity that has never been equaled, India's royalty developed an insatiable passion for gems.

A fable grew over the two thousand years that Indian dealers bought Egyptian emeralds from traders. Owners must have asked where the gems originated. Dealers apparently told them from an "Old Mine." This phrase and concept stuck in Indian gem lore until it had been ritualized into a real location. In his 1318 gem treatise, Indian writer Thakkur Ferru noted that Arab visitors to India as early as the ninth century mentioned emeralds. He related that one Arab, Al Idrissi, described an emerald mine located across the water on a hill with a desert beyond and a nearby village called Markat, a Sanskrit word for emerald. This certainly sounds like a description of Cleopatra's Mines in Egypt. Other Indian references recall the country's invasion by Persia's Alladin Khilji in the twelfth century, when invaders were said to have used camels to carry back emeralds. Those would have to have been Egyptian gems, if they were indeed emeralds.

Indian lore did not stop with the Old Mine reference as it pertained to a foreign source. Over the centuries as larger and finer emeralds entered the country and dealers either did not know or did not reveal where the gems originated, the Old Mine fable grew to become a lost mine fable. As I researched this book and my *National Geographic* article on emeralds, I found almost unlimited references to Old Mine gems. When I visited the grand old

families of gem owners, dealers, and cutters in Jaipur, every one of them firmly told me all the wonderful emerald treasures in public collections, those still hidden in private hands, the thousands of stones captured and transported to Iran (Persia) after Nadir Shah's sack of Delhi in 1739, and the great crystals in the Topkapi Palace Museum in Turkey were all originally emeralds from India's lost Old Mine.

Looking at the unsurpassed color and quality of pre-colonial material in India, such as the fobs on the opposite page and the beads on page 39, convinced me that Old Mine emeralds are actually Colombian. When I found telltale microscopic 3-phase inclusions indicative of Colombian emeralds, I was sure. Still, dealers who had been in the trade for nearly 70 years insisted these could not be from Colombia because their ancestors told them there really was an Old Mine and Indian writings from centuries before referred to Old Mine emeralds. Fables die hard.

I then set about to find any verifiable Indian drawing or painting older than 1500 A.D. that included a fine emerald. Having found none, I decided to collect as many gorgeous emeralds as possible in India, have reputable local dealers agree they were "Old Mine" stones, then ship them to one of the world's leading gem labs for examination. As I expected, they all tested as Colombian.

Once I had resolved the basic mystery, the facts appeared clear. India traded for Egyptian emeralds from perhaps 2000 or 3000 B.C. until that source was exhausted in the thirteenth century. There is always the possibility that a few gems also arrived from Pakistan, Afghanistan, or Russia over the millennia. But none of those sources had the size or look of the fabulous crystals that appeared once the Spanish conquered Colombia. Those early Colombian emeralds went directly to Spain. Since the Spanish had no particular fondness for emeralds nor a ready-made market such as already existed in the 1500s in India, they transshipped the jewels to Bombay. Later, as this trade matured and navigation and sailing skills improved, they innovated a short cut. Spain captured the Philippines, allowing its convoys to embark from the west coast of South America directly for Asia. This Pacific route led to the new Indian fable that emeralds were coming from yet another Old Mine, this time in Southeast Asia.

The world of emeralds changed dramatically once Colombia's treasures spread overseas. At once it was apparent to all just how large and beautiful emeralds could be. Completing the precious gem quartet with diamonds, rubies, and sapphires, these jewels that initially captivated potentates soon became global favorites.

Priceless relics from another age, this pair of Colombian emerald fobs once decorated a maharajah's scabbard. Gems of this size and quality are rarely mined today. Prior to independence and the breakup of royal estates, India was a prime market for important jewels.

SYNTHETIC EMERALDS; FAKES AND IMITATIONS

Humans have cherished two enduring dreams: to turn lead into gold and to transform ordinary chemicals into gems. Alas, the first remains elusive, but Auguste Verneuil made the second a reality when he synthesized rubies. Since the end of the eighteenth century, scientists and hobbyists have mastered one technique after another, experimenting on successive gems until they now grow all major gemstones.

The correct term for a laboratory-grown, man-made, "cultured," or "created" gem is *synthetic*—a material that has the same chemistry and properties as a natural crystal. Gem crystal growers dodge the term because common English usage of the word connotes fake or look-alike, but the accurate scientific definition of a created equivalent is indeed "synthetic."

Flame-fusion rubies electrified the gem world at the turn of the century, initially causing wild fluctuations before prices rapidly stabilized. Soon several firms began making synthetic sapphires and spinels by the extraordinarily simple flame-fusion process, which still accounts for the vast majority of the billion carats annual production of synthetic gems. Flame-fusion synthesis, a several hour process at most, works for only a few gem types; it does not work for emeralds.

CALIFORNIA DREAMER CARROLL CHATHAM, alone in his basement created the first synthetic emeralds in the 1930s. Naturally secretive, Chatham revealed his tiny crystals but not his process. In time he produced sufficient sizes and quantities to sell as Chatham Created Emeralds. He grew his crystals by the far more complicated and costly flux process, which recreates the earth's magma in a cauldron of molten material (the flux). To that glowing mass Chatham added emerald seed crystals, aluminum and silicon oxides, and beryllium. Keeping this brew for up to a year at near melting temperatures, Chatham created emeralds.

After Carroll's death, his son John greatly improved the crystal growing process. Carroll's other son Tom began a very successful marketing

Biron grows emeralds using the hydrothermal process. The Australian firm produced this incredibly clean, almost perfect specimen.

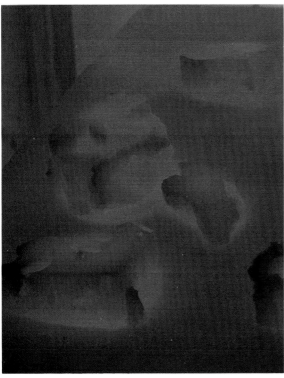

John Chatham grows most of the world's laboratory emeralds in San Francisco. Expanding on a procedure his father developed, Chatham has consistently increased the size and quality of the product. He uses the flux process, which takes nearly a year to produce crystals like these. Once he removes them from furnaces, John anneals the crystals with additional heating to make them more durable. Every aspect of the lab is secret; these are the first pictures ever allowed inside the Chatham laboratory.

Blue Planet Gems

Occasionally the flux process produces crystal clusters, useless to the Chathams as individual gems but sought by collectors and jewelry designers. This unusual gold pin contains over 200 carats of Chatham's emerald crystals that bonded together as they grew.

program by positioning prices between extremely inexpensive flame-fusion synthetics (rubies, sapphires, and spinels) and natural emeralds. The Chatham brothers routinely produce the majority of the world's gem quality synthetic emeralds. Judith Osmer, a Chatham competitor with her flux-grown rubies, says, "I think Chatham and I would have a market even if we priced at ten percent of naturals. But we're selling our synthetics at one to three percent the cost of naturals because their prices soared and ours didn't rise at all."

Chatham does have at least two serious synthetic emerald competitors, Biron in Australia and newly independent Russia. Biron makes large, almost inclusion-free synthetic emeralds by the hydrothermal process, very different from flux-grown. Duplicating underground conditions where Colombian emeralds formed, Biron places the chemical ingredients of emeralds and seed crystals into a water-filled pressure chamber. With the proper heat and pressure, remarkably clean synthetic emeralds over 100 carats grow in just a few weeks. Russia's gem crystal growing is an outgrowth of the former USSR's nuclear program. Russia produces both hydrothermal and flux-grown synthetic emeralds, now valued for hard currency.

In this case...
All That's Red
Is Emerald

Since there are so many emerald simulants, fakes, and imitations, the gem trade has a fast, inexpensive, and usually reliable means of separating the genuine from just green stones. The test is based on the fact that most emeralds are green because of trace amounts of chromium. Viewed through a Chelsea filter, developed in England, crystals containing chromium show up red. Imitations and simulants without chromium are dark.

In the white light picture above, two huge Biron hydrothermal synthetic emerald crystals flank a large cluster of chromium-rich Chatham flux-grown synthetic emeralds. Between them are 5 pale natural Madagascar emeralds. To the left of the Colombian natural emerald ring are 8 Biron synthetics. Above and to the right of the ring are 8 Chatham synthetics and at the far right, 5 Russian synthetics. In the view through a Chelsea filter (below), all the materials glowing red contain chromium. The others are either colored by vanadium or are too thick for light to pass. Fakes also show no red.

Both these stones look real (left), but only one is genuine. The imitation, a doublet, cost $10 on the street in Bogotá, but tourists usually pay much more, believing it is a natural. The truth is revealed in a side view (above) that shows a light glue line that typically bonds two pieces of synthetic spinel, glass, or quartz.

Though people rightly place a distinct premium on the rarity and beauty of natural gems, synthetics do have some advantages. Oiling is unnecessary, and they are less fragile and more deeply colored than most commercial grade naturals. With proper disclosure, synthetics fill a price niche that does not affect the market for natural emeralds.

BEWARE OF FAKES, IMITATIONS, AND SIMULANTS. There are thousands of green look-alikes that do not have the properties of emeralds. When marketed as inexpensive imitations for costume jewelry, they are legitimate, but too often dealers sell them to deceive. Real emeralds have a world price, so suspect any "bargain" advertised at "wholesale."

Glass, plastic, synthetic emeralds, or other natural green stones made up to look like emerald rough from a mine are usually peddled to unsuspecting buyers near real emerald mines and markets. Sometimes dissemblers cast genuine emerald crystals and mold realistic glass or plastic models, which they cake with dirt and sell at "bargain" prices. They are common in Third World countries and some mail order catalogs. Although almost any transparent green material can be cut to look like an emerald, gemologists can tell the difference. Do not buy anything that appears too good to be true. Buy gems only from someone you know and trust.

BUYING AND CARING

Afterall you decide to buy gems, your next most important considerations are where and how to choose them, then how to care for your
new treasures. By following a few simple guidelines, most buyers can
save money on exactly the gemstones or pieces of jewelry they want and assure
a lifetime of enjoyment. I recommend that you research buying a gem with
the same enthusiasm and care you might give to any other major purchase,
such as choosing a washing machine or car, which will probably cost less and
not last as long.

Buying gems and selecting designs can and should be satisfying, even
memorable experiences. To make you a knowledgeable consumer about a
variety of materials, each book in this gem series deals with a separate
gemstone. For the moment we will concentrate on emeralds, but you will see
that you can use the same general concepts when buying other colored gems.
Diamond pricing, color, and clarity are considerably more complicated. For
the average diamond consumer, imperceptibly small differences in color and
clarity cause vast price differences. A diamond buyer will benefit from the
assistance of an expert, but with an hour of comparative shopping, you can
learn to choose an emerald competently. In many ways, buying emeralds is
easier than buying other gemstones simply because, with emeralds, you
usually get what you see.

The same basic characteristics of color, clarity, carat weight, and cut
that determine diamond values also work for emeralds and other colored
gemstones, but the emphasis is on different factors. With diamonds, unless
you move all the way to definitely colored (called fancy) diamonds, the less
color in the stone the better. With emeralds, it is exactly the opposite.

Color is everything. There has to be a perfect balance—darker than
peridot and lighter than tourmaline. The purer and more brilliant the

*Color, clarity, and carat weight are the keys to emerald prices. To
sharpen their judgment, smart buyers comparison shop to master the
nuances of emerald quality. Small changes in the depth of color can cause
huge swings in costs. Being a discriminating buyer pays.*

Blue Planet Gems/John Troha (3)

Roditi Jewelers

A fine suite of matched emeralds is rare and expensive because of the difficulty in assembling quality colored gems with similar sizes, color, and shapes. This Zambian emerald necklace was handmade in Brazil.

emerald, the more it costs. As emerald dealer Maurice Shire says, "The cardinal sin of any emerald is not being green."

Carat weight considerations are somewhat similar to those for diamonds and other gems, but colored stones take a smaller leap in prices if they weigh precisely an even carat or more. Diamonds make big price jumps at one carat, at two carats , etc. Large emeralds, which are rare, increase in price faster, but more proportionately. As emerald weights double, their prices often quadruple. Clean emeralds over three carats with good color command premium prices, typically higher than comparable diamonds.

Clarity in emeralds differs from other gems. Remember, as Type III gems, emeralds are the only major gemstone expected to have visible inclusions; in fact, any specimen without them is immediately suspect as a synthetic or an imitation. Still, inclusions do affect price. If all other factors are equal, the natural emerald with the fewest inclusions is the most valuable.

Gemologists grade all stones at 10 power magnification. Unlike diamond's flawless designation, the top GIA colored stone clarity grade is VVS (Very Very Slightly Included). Each of the three gem types has its own criteria. For emeralds, Type III gems, VVS describes the highest of seven grades—gems with inclusions that are noticeable at 10X but usually invisible to the unaided eye.

In the year and a half I spent researching and doing field work on

Good jewelry is timeless. Fads may change, but quality is always in style. Buy well and your grandchildren will be wearing your purchases in the next century. With emeralds, clean stones are stronger. Buy the best color and clarity you can afford.

emeralds, I saw only one natural emerald that surpassed VVS, a 14 carat pear-shaped beauty with less than perfect color. Even so, it was priced at wholesale for one million dollars, entirely because of its clarity. Recalling the earlier discussion on oiling, you can be certain that all emeralds are soaked in oil during their storage and processing. Whether or not oiling is done after cutting depends on inclusions reaching the stone's surfaces. If they do, presume your emerald is oiled. Realize that the gem probably has more inclusions than you can see, and it should be reoiled every 2-5 years. Its price and value are barely affected, despite what you may be told. Color, size, and the number and types of inclusions mainly determine value.

Here is where comparisons pay. Go to a few jewelry stores to look carefully at emeralds. A reputable dealer will show comparative gems. Avoid any with enough inclusions to give the stone a "sleepy" or subdued appearance. Notice the difference between bright, deep green emeralds and lighter, duller commercial grades. Ask to see emeralds that sell for $10,000 a carat. Before you leave the counter, commit to memory characteristics that make expensive emeralds worth the price.

Using Colombian emeralds as a constant, compare their color with emeralds from Zambia and Brazil. The price differential is normally not as great as Burma rubies command over Thai or African rubies. Still, Colombian emeralds usually sell for a ten to twenty percent premium. If you pay such a premium, make sure you can see the difference.

Cut, or "make," of a gem is important to its overall appearance. Greater precision produces more beautifully proportioned gems with greater life and sparkle. Buyers demand well cut diamonds, but the gem trade and ultimately consumers accept wide variations in colored stone cutting quality. Third World cutters hand facet most emeralds. Since gems are sold by the carat, they have a tendency to cut first for weight, then for beauty.

Old and new jewels work beautifully together. In India, where banking remains uncommon, women traditionally wear their wealth, displaying both dowry and savings. Indians hand down gems through generations, an increasingly popular idea with Americans. Buy quality gems and jewelry that will last, so you can enjoy them for decades before passing legacies to children and grandchildren.

Owners worry about the safety of their emeralds. Be aware that emeralds and all other gems (even diamonds) can break. But emeralds are much more durable than softer jewels such as opals, pearls, coral, or tanzanite. At 71/2 to 8 on the Mohs hardness scale (where diamonds are 10), emeralds are harder than most steel.

When a stone is heavily included or has serious inclusions reaching the surface, it can be damaged by a goldsmith's torch or by a sharp blow. Therefore, use only goldsmiths experienced with emeralds. Owners seldom have difficulties with prong-set earrings or pins. If you are particularly rough on jewelry, you may want to bezel or channel set emeralds in a bracelet. Because ring emeralds are especially vulnerable, I strongly suggest you choose a bezel setting for extra protection.

Always remove fine jewelry before heavy activities, washing dishes by hand, or working with tools. A hard knock against a stainless steel sink, for instance, can break a diamond, ruby, or emerald.

Clean your emeralds with warm water and a mild soap or detergent. You can also use alcohol or vodka with a soft toothbrush. Never put your emeralds into ultrasonic cleaners or steamers, which might remove internal oil and break stones. Avoid rapid temperature changes and high heat. Your emeralds have survived the rigors of a tumultuous formation in molten rock and are already millions of years old. They are, after all, considerably more durable than humans. My best advice is to relax and enjoy owning and wearing emeralds. They are royal jewels, fit for a king, or a queen.

Advantages of Emeralds

Color—green is a calm, soothing, appealing hue; the color of
    youth, spring, the symbol of the earth and of self-reliance
Rarity—among highest investment values of all gems
Durability—hard, but not as tough as diamond or rubies
Weight—larger than other gems at the same weight
History—one of the longest and grandest of any gem
Birthstone—May

Caring for Emeralds

Home cleaning—warm water; mild detergent; alcohol with soft brush.
Ultrasonic or Steamer—not safe. Either technique can result in breakage as
well as inadvertently removing oils used to mask inclusions.
Setting—should be undertaken only by skilled workers. Above all other
major gemstones, emeralds should be set and reset only by people experienced with the special handling requirements of emeralds.
Storing—to prevent scratching, store separately from diamonds and other
harder gems. Velvet-lined boxes with individual compartments are best.
Reoiling—replace original oil every 2 to 5 years.

Sugar-loaf cabochon and natural crystal, Equatorian Imports, Dallas   Ring, Harry Winston, Inc., New York

*Emeralds await your every wish. For crystal collectors, specimen as fine as this
10.86 carat rod from Colombia's Chivor mine, are rare treasures. The 26 carat
sugar-loaf cabochon, fit for a queen, will likely be set in a pin or pendant. And the
classic 8.90 carat Colombian emerald ring, accented with diamond trillions, is
always in style. All three will appreciate, because they are all beautiful and rare.*

Gemstones are sold by weight, not by size or volume. This significant difference makes them more like gold and silver than other luxury products, such as furs, yachts, automobiles, or watches. Since gems are comprised of different chemical elements, they do not all weigh the same. Therefore, gemologists use weight as one means of identification.

Weight, or density, is expressed as specific gravity (SG). Diamond has an SG of 3.52, which means a diamond weighs 3.52 times as much as the same volume of water. Emeralds are lighter, with an SG of 2.72, nearly the same as quartz and pearls. Because gems vary so much in specific gravity, their sizes vary considerably compared with other gems of the same weight. With emeralds you get a bigger jewel for the same weight as other major gems.

Gems are weighed in carats (not to be confused with *karat*, which refers to the purity of gold). A carat, from the ancient Indian use of carob seeds for small consistent weights, equals 1/5 gram, or 1/142 ounce. Sizes are measured in millimeters (see below). A round one carat emerald, a standard weight in the trade, is typically 6.6mm in diameter. A round one carat ruby or sapphire, being denser, measures 6.1mm across. So, a one carat emerald is physically larger than a similarly cut one carat diamond or ruby.

Cutting proportions vary far more in colored stones than diamonds, especially from Third World cutters. When buying, the main considerations after color and clarity are the quality of the cutting and the final proportions. Beauty is a major component in the "make" of a colored gem.

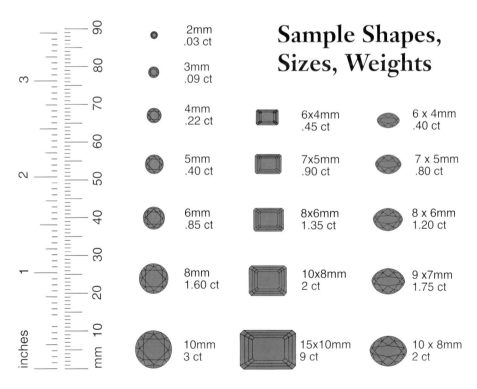

Sample Shapes, Sizes, Weights

2mm	.03 ct
3mm	.09 ct
4mm	.22 ct
5mm	.40 ct
6mm	.85 ct
8mm	1.60 ct
10mm	3 ct

6x4mm	.45 ct
7x5mm	.90 ct
8x6mm	1.35 ct
10x8mm	2 ct
15x10mm	9 ct

6 x 4mm	.40 ct
7 x 5mm	.80 ct
8 x 6mm	1.20 ct
9 x7mm	1.75 ct
10 x 8mm	2 ct

Approximate weights of round, emerald cut, and oval emeralds in a variety of sizes.

Colombia continues to set the color and quality standards for emeralds. Unlike other producing locations, most of Colombia's gems are cut within the country. Emeralds of this color and clarity typically sell for several thousand dollars a carat in any of these popular shapes.